MAD LIBS JUNIOR™

SCHOOL RULES!
MAD LIBS JUNIOR

By Roger Price and Leonard Stern

PSS!
PRICE STERN SLOAN

ISBN 978-0-8431-0853-8

First Edition
9 10

MAD LIBS JUNIOR
INSTRUCTIONS

MAD LIBS JUNIOR™ is a game for kids who don't like games! It can be played by one, two, three, four, or forty.

RIDICULOUSLY SIMPLE DIRECTIONS:

At the top of each page in this book, you will find four columns of words, each headed by a symbol. Each symbol represents a part of speech. The symbols are:

★ NOUNS

⬤ ADJECTIVES

↑ VERBS

? MISC.

MAD LIBS JUNIOR™ is fun to play with friends, but you can also play it by yourself! To begin, look at the story on the page below. When you come to a blank space in the story, look at the symbol that appears underneath. Then find the same symbol on this page and pick a word that appears below the symbol. Put that word in the blank space, and cross out the word, so you don't use it again. Continue doing this throughout the story until you've filled in all the spaces. Finally, read your story aloud and laugh!

EXAMPLE:

"Good-bye!" he said, as he jumped into his _____ and _____
                           ⬤   ?
off with his pet _____.
               ★

★ NOUNS	⬤ ADJECTIVES	↑ VERBS	? MISC.
hamster	curly	drove	car
dog	purple	~~danced~~	boat
cat	wet	drank	roller skate
~~giraffe~~	tired	twirled	taxicab
monkey	silly	swam	~~surfboard~~

"Good-bye!" he said, as he jumped into his _SURFBOARD_ and _DANCED_
                           ⬤   ?
off with his pet _GIRAFFE_.
               ★

MAD LIBS JUNIOR

QUICK REVIEW

In case you haven't learned about the parts of speech yet, here is a quick lesson:

A NOUN ★ is the name of a person, place, or thing. *Sidewalk, umbrella, bathtub,* and *roller blades* are nouns.

An ADJECTIVE ☺ describes a person, place, or thing. *Lumpy, soft, ugly, messy,* and *short* are adjectives.

A VERB ➜ is an action word. *Run, jump,* and *swim* are verbs.

MISC. ? will be any word that does not apply to the other categories. Some examples of a word that could be miscellaneous are: *part of the body, animal, number, color,* and *a place.*

MAD LIBS JUNIOR™ is fun to play with friends, but you can also play it by yourself! To begin, look at the story on the page below. When you come to a blank space in the story, look at the symbol that appears underneath. Then find the same symbol on this page and pick a word that appears below the symbol. Put that word in the blank space, and cross out the word, so you don't use it again. Continue doing this throughout the story until you've filled in all the spaces. Finally, read your story aloud and laugh!

FIRST DAY OF SCHOOL

★ NOUNS	🐷 ADJECTIVES	➡ VERBS	❓ MISC.
sardines	nasty	dance	pink
waffles	great	fart	yellow
pencils	funny	cry	green
sausages	slimy	burp	brown
eggs	gross	sing	blue
pickles	cool	scream	purple
apples	hairy	moan	white
noodles	sick	jump	orange
worms	dumb	skip	gray
jelly beans	silly	shake	black
muffins	goofy	run	red
monkeys	stinky	leap	silver

MAD LIBS JUNIOR

FIRST DAY OF SCHOOL

On the first day of school, I felt so _____ . I put on my

favorite new outfit—a shirt with two _____ (☺) _____ ★

on it and a _____ (☺) _____ ? pair of pants. My mom made

me my favorite breakfast, _____ ? _____ ★ and pancakes. My brother

told me my new teacher was really _____ (☺) . He had her last

year and said she lets kids _____ ↑ in class. When the big

_____ ? bus pulled up outside, I waved good-bye to my mom,

who started to _____ ↑ . I got a seat with my friend Pete, who

showed me his new _____ ? backpack that was full of

_____ ↑ . When I finally got to school, I was so excited that I

started to _____ ★ in the hallway. I think this is going to be a

really _____ (☺) year!

From School Rules! Mad Libs Junior™ • Copyright 2004 by Price Stern Sloan,
a division of Penguin Young Readers Group, 345 Hudson Street, New York, NY 10014.

MAD LIBS JUNIOR™ is fun to play with friends, but you can also play it by yourself! To begin, look at the story on the page below. When you come to a blank space in the story, look at the symbol that appears underneath. Then find the same symbol on this page and pick a word that appears below the symbol. Put that word in the blank space, and cross out the word, so you don't use it again. Continue doing this throughout the story until you've filled in all the spaces. Finally, read your story aloud and laugh!

OUR CAFETERIA

★ NOUNS	😊 ADJECTIVES	↑ VERBS	? MISC.
shoes	horrible	wiggle	purple
goats	tasty	jump	brown
tires	gross	growl	green
snails	delicious	dance	yellow
socks	yummy	scream	red
mushrooms	nasty	move	blue
rubber bands	slimy	sing	pink
snakes	furry	shiver	orange
bananas	lumpy	crawl	tan
cheese	chewy	shake	silver
mothballs	slippery	squirm	white
tuna fish	squishy	cry	gray

MAD LIBS JUNIOR

OUR CAFETERIA

Our school cafeteria has really _____ food. Just thinking about it makes my stomach _____ . The spaghetti is _____ and tastes like _____ ★. One day, I swear one of my meatballs started to _____ ↑! The turkey tacos are totally _____ ⊕ and look kind of like old _____. My friend Dana actually likes the meatloaf, even though it's _____ and _____ ⊕. I call it "mystery meatloaf" and think it's really made out of _____ ★. My dad said he'd make my lunches, but the first day, he made me a sandwich out of _____ ★ and peanut butter! I think I'd rather take my chances with the cafeteria!

From School Rules! Mad Libs Junior™ • Copyright 2004 by Price Stern Sloan,
a division of Penguin Young Readers Group, 345 Hudson Street, New York, NY 10014.

MAD LIBS JUNIOR™ is fun to play with friends, but you can also play it by yourself! To begin, look at the story on the page below. When you come to a blank space in the story, look at the symbol that appears underneath. Then find the same symbol on this page and pick a word that appears below the symbol. Put that word in the blank space, and cross out the word, so you don't use it again. Continue doing this throughout the story until you've filled in all the spaces. Finally, read your story aloud and laugh!

CLASS PET

★ NOUNS	☺ ADJECTIVES	↑ VERBS	? MISC.
octopus	smelly	burps	orange
rock	fun	talks	green
turtle	hairy	sings	purple
hamster	goofy	reads	pink
pig	stinky	laughs	red
monkey	funny	yells	blue
hyena	boring	dances	black
frog	gross	jumps	brown
dinosaur	silly	farts	white
elephant	nasty	giggles	gray
slug	chubby	runs	yellow
bat	quiet	screams	silver

MAD LIBS JUNIOR

CLASS PET

Our class has a pet, a/an _____ _____ named
? ★

Scooter. I think Scooter is really _____. Mostly, he
😎

just hangs around and _____, but sometimes he
➡

_____ like a/an _____. When Scooter gets
➡ ★

scared, he turns bright _____. I know, because one day I
?

held a/an _____ up to his cage and it scared him.
★

Sometimes, Scooter _____ in the middle of class and
➡

the whole class stops to watch him. Having a class pet sure is

_____. I told my parents I'd like a big _____
😎 😎

_____ for a pet at home. That'd be much better than a
★

_____ little sister!
😎

MAD LIBS JUNIOR™ is fun to play with friends, but you can also play it by yourself! To begin, look at the story on the page below. When you come to a blank space in the story, look at the symbol that appears underneath. Then find the same symbol on this page and pick a word that appears below the symbol. Put that word in the blank space, and cross out the word, so you don't use it again. Continue doing this throughout the story until you've filled in all the spaces. Finally, read your story aloud and laugh!

FAKING SICK

★ NOUNS	😊 ADJECTIVES	→ VERBS	? MISC.
ox	nasty	scream	purple
gerbil	big	laugh	brown
clam	ugly	cry	green
alien	yucky	sneeze	yellow
toad	silly	moan	red
squid	dumb	gasp	blue
horse	bumpy	sniffle	pink
germ	healthy	yell	orange
potato	slimy	cough	tan
chicken	happy	burp	silver
pumpkin	sick	snort	white
monkey	pretty	fart	gray

MAD LIBS JUNIOR

FAKING SICK

One day, we were going to have a big _____ test at school,

so I decided to fake sick and stay home. My best friend had just

gotten the _____ pox and that gave me an idea. I got a/an

_____ magic marker and drew spots all over my skin. Then I

started to _____ and called for my mom. When my mom

came in my room, I started to cough and _____ really

loudly. But my mom just said, "You look as _____ as a/an

_____ to me. Get dressed for school! And scrub those

_____ dots off your skin, too." When I got my test score back

the next day, I really did feel sick!

MAD LIBS JUNIOR™ is fun to play with friends, but you can also play it by yourself! To begin, look at the story on the page below. When you come to a blank space in the story, look at the symbol that appears underneath. Then find the same symbol on this page and pick a word that appears below the symbol. Put that word in the blank space, and cross out the word, so you don't use it again. Continue doing this throughout the story until you've filled in all the spaces. Finally, read your story aloud and laugh!

OUR PRINCIPAL

★	☺	➡	?
NOUNS	**ADJECTIVES**	**VERBS**	**MISC.**
mothballs	ugly	spit	purple
pickles	silly	burp	brown
onions	nasty	grunt	blue
eggs	goofy	fart	green
french fries	funny	laugh	orange
peas	slimy	snort	red
mushrooms	hairy	dance	gray
sardines	old	sneeze	pink
cookies	smelly	shake	navy blue
beans	fancy	giggle	silver
olives	dirty	cry	white
acorns	messy	wiggle	black

Our principal, Mr. Picklestick, is really _____. He has

two _____ moles on his chin that look just like

_____. They have big _____ hairs sprouting out

of them and they wiggle when he talks. His breath smells like wet

_____ and whenever he yells at a student, he starts to

_____. He also has little, beady _____ eyes that

watch your every move. My friend Dante got in trouble because he

started to _____ in the hallway and he had to go to Mr.

Picklestick's office. He said he made him clean his _____

desk while he sat there eating _____. I hope I never have to

go to his office!

MAD LIBS JUNIOR™ is fun to play with friends, but you can also play it by yourself! To begin, look at the story on the page below. When you come to a blank space in the story, look at the symbol that appears underneath. Then find the same symbol on this page and pick a word that appears below the symbol. Put that word in the blank space, and cross out the word, so you don't use it again. Continue doing this throughout the story until you've filled in all the spaces. Finally, read your story aloud and laugh!

TEACHER TROUBLE

★ NOUNS	☻ ADJECTIVES	➡ VERBS	? MISC.
elephant	slimy	talk	purple
skateboard	smelly	sneeze	brown
monkey	ugly	laugh	green
computer	goofy	fart	yellow
football	mean	scream	red
train	hyper	snort	blue
sweater	silly	burp	pink
toothbrush	dumb	giggle	orange
radio	wild	clap	tan
baseball	nosy	sing	silver
bike	tough	dance	white
surfboard	nasty	jump	gray

MAD LIBS JUNIOR
TEACHER TROUBLE

I think my teacher Ms. Prune is _____ and doesn't like me.

She says I'm way too _____ and she turns _____

and starts to _____ every time I raise my hand. She made

my parents come in for a conference and told them I act like a/an

_____ _____. They were so mad, they took

away my brand-new _____. And the other day, she made me

stay after class and write, "I will not _____ in class" fifty

times on the blackboard with a piece of chalk the size of a/an

_____. Ms. Prune is _____!

MAD LIBS JUNIOR™ is fun to play with friends, but you can also play it by yourself! To begin, look at the story on the page below. When you come to a blank space in the story, look at the symbol that appears underneath. Then find the same symbol on this page and pick a word that appears below the symbol. Put that word in the blank space, and cross out the word, so you don't use it again. Continue doing this throughout the story until you've filled in all the spaces. Finally, read your story aloud and laugh!

BOOK REPORT

★ NOUNS	😀 ADJECTIVES	➡ VERBS	? MISC.
hamsters	boring	burp	black
toilets	stupid	sing	red
dinosaurs	funny	hunt	purple
butterflies	bad	eat	orange
sharks	cool	sleep	navy blue
spiders	neat	cook	gold
monsters	silly	dance	yellow
snails	awesome	fart	brown
poodles	horrible	swim	silver
pirates	dumb	play	pink
rabbits	goofy	breathe	lime green
aliens	dull	whistle	white

For my book report, I read a really _____ book about ☺

_____ . Did you know that their skin is _____ ?

and that they can grow up to twelve feet long? They are related to pre-

historic _____ . They love to eat _____ and they

only _____ ➡ at night. During the day, they live in the

water, but at night they climb trees to _____ ➡. They have

_____ ? eyes that they only close when they

_____ ➡. When the babies hatch from eggs, they look like

_____ _____ ? ★. I think I know every _____ ☺

fact there is to know about them. I bet my teacher will think my book

report is really _____ ! ☺

MAD LIBS JUNIOR™ is fun to play with friends, but you can also play it by yourself! To begin, look at the story on the page below. When you come to a blank space in the story, look at the symbol that appears underneath. Then find the same symbol on this page and pick a word that appears below the symbol. Put that word in the blank space, and cross out the word, so you don't use it again. Continue doing this throughout the story until you've filled in all the spaces. Finally, read your story aloud and laugh!

SHOW-AND-TELL

★	☺	➡	?
NOUNS	**ADJECTIVES**	**VERBS**	**MISC.**
map	cool	laughing	purple
television	dumb	yelling	brown
sandwich	strange	booing	green
banana	awesome	burping	yellow
shoe	slimy	snorting	red
potato	smelly	giggling	blue
golf ball	weird	crying	pink
pickle	crazy	choking	orange
sock	stinky	gagging	tan
ham	goofy	pointing	silver
lunch box	gross	sniffing	white
pizza	nasty	farting	gray

MAD LIBS JUNIOR
SHOW-AND-TELL

My family went to the beach and my dad and I found an old

_____ . I thought it was really _____ , so I took it

⭐   😊

to school for show-and-tell. I told my class that it had probably belonged

to a pirate like _____ Beard. He was really _____

❓   😊

and had a _____ for a hand, because he lost one in a sword

⭐

fight. I also said that he probably buried a _____ on the

⭐

beach, too. The other kids all started _____ and said it was

➡️

really _____ . My face turned bright _____ and I

😊   ❓

started _____ as I sat down. Next time, I think I'll just bring

➡️

a/an _____ _____ instead!

😊   ⭐

MAD LIBS JUNIOR™ is fun to play with friends, but you can also play it by yourself! To begin, look at the story on the page below. When you come to a blank space in the story, look at the symbol that appears underneath. Then find the same symbol on this page and pick a word that appears below the symbol. Put that word in the blank space, and cross out the word, so you don't use it again. Continue doing this throughout the story until you've filled in all the spaces. Finally, read your story aloud and laugh!

SCHOOL BUS RULES

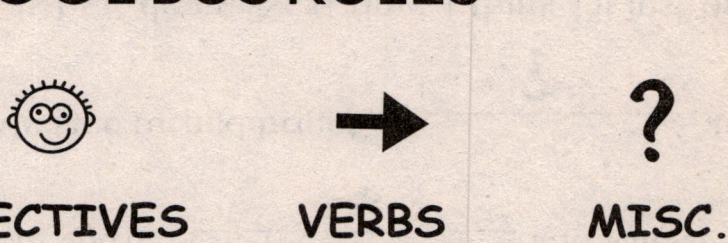

★ NOUNS	😀 ADJECTIVES	→ VERBS	? MISC.
firecrackers	stinky	singing	white
pickles	mean	laughing	blue
rocks	silly	running	black
sardines	nasty	farting	gold
hot dogs	bad	yelling	red
cupcakes	friendly	jumping	purple
goldfish	goofy	burping	pink
pumpkins	ugly	stomping	orange
yo-yos	evil	sneezing	brown
underwear	nice	screaming	turquoise
lizards	dangerous	playing	gray
socks	long	dancing	green

1. No _____ is allowed on the school bus. It could distract

   ➡️

   the driver and cause an accident.

2. Do not bring any _____ onto the school bus, unless they

   ⭐

   are packed away in your backpack.

3. No yelling, name-calling, or saying _____ words to other

   ☺

   students on the school bus.

4. Don't throw _____ at anyone on the school bus. They

   ⭐

   could hit another student and give them a/an _____ eye.

   ❓

5. Keep your _____ inside the school bus at all times.

   ⭐

   Never dangle them out the windows.

MAD LIBS JUNIOR™ is fun to play with friends, but you can also play it by yourself! To begin, look at the story on the page below. When you come to a blank space in the story, look at the symbol that appears underneath. Then find the same symbol on this page and pick a word that appears below the symbol. Put that word in the blank space, and cross out the word, so you don't use it again. Continue doing this throughout the story until you've filled in all the spaces. Finally, read your story aloud and laugh!

REPORT CARDS

★	😀	➡	?
NOUNS	**ADJECTIVES**	**VERBS**	**MISC.**
horse	dumb	kicking	pink
raccoon	horrible	smelling	yellow
octopus	wonderful	sniffing	green
monkey	silly	licking	brown
flower	goofy	tickling	blue
snake	stinky	hugging	purple
cactus	stupid	rubbing	white
monster	yucky	punching	orange
ostrich	nasty	kissing	gray
tiger	bad	squeezing	black
piglet	awesome	biting	red
rabbit	gross	petting	silver

English	A+
Math	A
Science	A
History	A
Art	A
P.E.	

MAD LIBS JUNIOR
REPORT CARDS

On Wednesday, we got our _____ report cards. Getting a

report card is about as fun as _____ a/an _____.

As usual, my teacher said my behavior is _____. She thinks I

act just like a wild _____. I think she's _____

and smells like a/an _____. My best friend Jack is really

_____, so he always gets good grades. Whenever he opens

his report card, he gets a big _____ smile on his face and he

starts _____ the report card. My parents said that if I got

good grades, they'd buy me a new _____. I really want a big

_____ one, but it looks like I'll have to wait for my birthday!

MAD LIBS JUNIOR™ is fun to play with friends, but you can also play it by yourself! To begin, look at the story on the page below. When you come to a blank space in the story, look at the symbol that appears underneath. Then find the same symbol on this page and pick a word that appears below the symbol. Put that word in the blank space, and cross out the word, so you don't use it again. Continue doing this throughout the story until you've filled in all the spaces. Finally, read your story aloud and laugh!

MUSIC CLASS

★	☺	→	?
NOUNS	**ADJECTIVES**	**VERBS**	**MISC.**
donkey	sick	sing	pink
pumpkin	stinky	cry	yellow
parrot	nice	yell	green
toilet	wild	laugh	brown
tree	horrible	whistle	blue
weasel	angry	fart	purple
scarecrow	cool	dance	white
witch	hairy	burp	orange
acorn	scary	cheer	gray
bird	dumb	clap	black
troll	silly	fly	red
cat	goofy	jump	silver

MAD LIBS ⊙ JUNIOR™
MUSIC CLASS

I love music class—it's my favorite place to _____ ➡ besides

the shower. Our teacher is a small lady with _____ ❓ hair who

looks like a/an _____ ⭐. She loves to _____ ➡ along

to the music. I think she's really _____ 😊 because she told me

I sing just like a/an _____ 😊 _____ ⭐. For our big fall

concert, we dressed up in _____ ❓ turtlenecks and sang a song

about a/an _____ ⭐ that liked to _____ ➡. I had a

solo where I had to _____ ➡ onstage all by myself. When the

concert was over, I took a bow and everyone in the audience started to

_____ ➡—especially my parents!

MAD LIBS JUNIOR™ is fun to play with friends, but you can also play it by yourself! To begin, look at the story on the page below. When you come to a blank space in the story, look at the symbol that appears underneath. Then find the same symbol on this page and pick a word that appears below the symbol. Put that word in the blank space, and cross out the word, so you don't use it again. Continue doing this throughout the story until you've filled in all the spaces. Finally, read your story aloud and laugh!

FIELD TRIP

★ NOUNS	😊 ADJECTIVES	➡ VERBS	? MISC.
cucumbers	crazy	feeding	purple
cupcakes	sick	riding	brown
lemons	dumb	wrestling	green
pencils	rubbery	tickling	yellow
lollipops	slimy	catching	red
potato chips	wild	sniffing	blue
socks	greasy	petting	pink
pickles	wet	washing	orange
doughnuts	squishy	hugging	tan
sponges	silly	chasing	silver
carrots	slippery	kissing	white
peanuts	stinky	biting	gray

MAD LIBS JUNIOR
FIELD TRIP

On Tuesday, our class went on a really _____ field trip to

the aquarium. We saw some very weird fish that looked like

_____ with fins on them. There was a diver in one tank who

started _____ a shark. What a _____ thing to do!

My favorite part of the aquarium was the touch tank, where I touched

two _____ sea _____. They felt like _____

_____. The dolphin show was also really cool. Dolphins are

big _____ creatures that are really _____.

These dolphins jumped up and grabbed _____ right out of

people's mouths. Then they started _____ fish when the

trainer blew his whistle. I sure wish I had a pet dolphin!

MAD LIBS JUNIOR™ is fun to play with friends, but you can also play it by yourself! To begin, look at the story on the page below. When you come to a blank space in the story, look at the symbol that appears underneath. Then find the same symbol on this page and pick a word that appears below the symbol. Put that word in the blank space, and cross out the word, so you don't use it again. Continue doing this throughout the story until you've filled in all the spaces. Finally, read your story aloud and laugh!

CLASS PLAY

★	☺	➡	?
NOUNS	**ADJECTIVES**	**VERBS**	**MISC.**
wizard	ugly	laugh	black
tree	smelly	fart	red
king	awesome	cough	purple
wolf	stiff	giggle	orange
butterfly	fuzzy	burp	navy blue
knight	goofy	drool	gold
turtle	shiny	sneeze	yellow
lion	boring	snort	brown
dragon	slimy	sweat	silver
elf	silly	dance	pink
toad	funny	barf	lime green
troll	hairy	sing	white

Our class is going to put on a/an _____ play. It's about a kind,

old _____ who falls under a/an _____ spell cast

by a wicked _____. The spell makes him _____

and turns him _____. The spell can't be broken until he

is kissed by a/an _____. I tried out for the part of the

_____, but the teacher said that I was too _____

for that role. He said I could play a/an _____ instead. My mom

is making me a costume out of some _____ _____

fabric she had leftover from making curtains. With that and some

_____ tights, I think I'll look really _____.

I can't wait!

MAD LIBS JUNIOR™ is fun to play with friends, but you can also play it by yourself! To begin, look at the story on the page below. When you come to a blank space in the story, look at the symbol that appears underneath. Then find the same symbol on this page and pick a word that appears below the symbol. Put that word in the blank space, and cross out the word, so you don't use it again. Continue doing this throughout the story until you've filled in all the spaces. Finally, read your story aloud and laugh!

CLASS ELECTION SPEECH

★	☺	→	?
NOUNS	**ADJECTIVES**	**VERBS**	**MISC.**
hot dogs	silly	jumping	gold
gerbils	stupid	fighting	aqua
cupcakes	fuzzy	talking	yellow
pumpkins	goofy	burping	beige
french fries	wacky	sleeping	black
peas	good	running	white
sardines	crazy	laughing	pink
dumplings	bad	singing	green
crackers	funny	dancing	red
fish sticks	dumb	farting	purple
biscuits	furry	screaming	blue
onions	ugly	napping	silver

MAD LIBS JUNIOR
CLASS ELECTION SPEECH

"Good morning, teachers, _____, and fellow students. You

may have seen my _____ _____ posters in the

hallway, and I'm here today to tell you all the _____ reasons

why you should vote for me for class president. If I was president, I would

have the school painted _____ and change our mascots to

the _____ _____. If I was president, teachers

would allow _____ in the classroom. We would also have

_____ for lunch every Friday. Finally, you should vote for me

because I love _____ as much as you do. So on voting

day remember to stop _____ and vote for me, the

_____ choice for president!"

MAD LIBS JUNIOR™ is fun to play with friends, but you can also play it by yourself! To begin, look at the story on the page below. When you come to a blank space in the story, look at the symbol that appears underneath. Then find the same symbol on this page and pick a word that appears below the symbol. Put that word in the blank space, and cross out the word, so you don't use it again. Continue doing this throughout the story until you've filled in all the spaces. Finally, read your story aloud and laugh!

MORNING ANNOUNCEMENTS

★ NOUNS	☺ ADJECTIVES	➡ VERBS	? MISC.
banana	smelly	running	purple
monkey	goofy	singing	brown
fish	ugly	farting	green
hippo	silly	dancing	yellow
spinach	stinky	sleeping	red
sardine	happy	skipping	blue
mustard	boring	burping	pink
jellyfish	super	flying	orange
potato	dumb	jumping	tan
octopus	wacky	talking	silver
pickle	dorky	cooking	white
liver	funny	painting	gray

MAD LIBS ⊙ JUNIOR
MORNING ANNOUNCEMENTS

"Good morning, students. This is your _____ principal,

Miss _____ . We have a few _____ announcements

this morning:

• The _____ club will have its first meeting today—anyone

interested in joining should bring their _____ and meet in the

library at three o'clock. All _____ students are welcome.

• For lunch today, the cafeteria will be serving _____

sandwiches on _____ bread with french fries and

_____ gelatin for dessert.

• Finally, please remember that _____ is not allowed in the hallways

or the library unless you have a/an _____ pass from your teacher.

• Thanks for your attention—have a/an _____ day!"

From School Rules! Mad Libs Junior™ • Copyright 2004 by Price Stern Sloan,
a division of Penguin Young Readers Group, 345 Hudson Street, New York, NY 10014.

MAD LIBS JUNIOR™ is fun to play with friends, but you can also play it by yourself! To begin, look at the story on the page below. When you come to a blank space in the story, look at the symbol that appears underneath. Then find the same symbol on this page and pick a word that appears below the symbol. Put that word in the blank space, and cross out the word, so you don't use it again. Continue doing this throughout the story until you've filled in all the spaces. Finally, read your story aloud and laugh!

THE LIBRARY

★ NOUNS	☺ ADJECTIVES	➡ VERBS	? MISC.
aliens	old	laugh	pink
dinosaurs	ugly	burp	yellow
toilets	funny	scream	green
teachers	smelly	cough	brown
rats	boring	giggle	blue
trash	silly	sneeze	purple
turtles	scary	fart	white
chickens	stinky	blink	orange
flowers	bad	snore	gray
hamsters	cool	yell	black
cars	dumb	snort	red
clowns	dorky	cry	silver

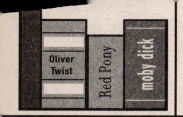

MAD LIBS JUNIOR

THE LIBRARY

I like to go to the school library because it's really _____ and

it's full of _____. I think the library smells just like old

_____—it must be from all the books. I always check out

books about _____—they're my favorite. I thinks books are

_____. You have to be very quiet in the library and you can't

_____ in it. The librarian says it should be so quiet that you

could hear a mouse _____. She's a/an _____

woman with _____ hair. Once a week, she reads to us from

a really _____ book. She always starts to _____

during the _____ parts.

MAD LIBS JUNIOR™ is fun to play with friends, but you can also play it by yourself! To begin, look at the story on the page below. When you come to a blank space in the story, look at the symbol that appears underneath. Then find the same symbol on this page and pick a word that appears below the symbol. Put that word in the blank space, and cross out the word, so you don't use it again. Continue doing this throughout the story until you've filled in all the spaces. Finally, read your story aloud and laugh!

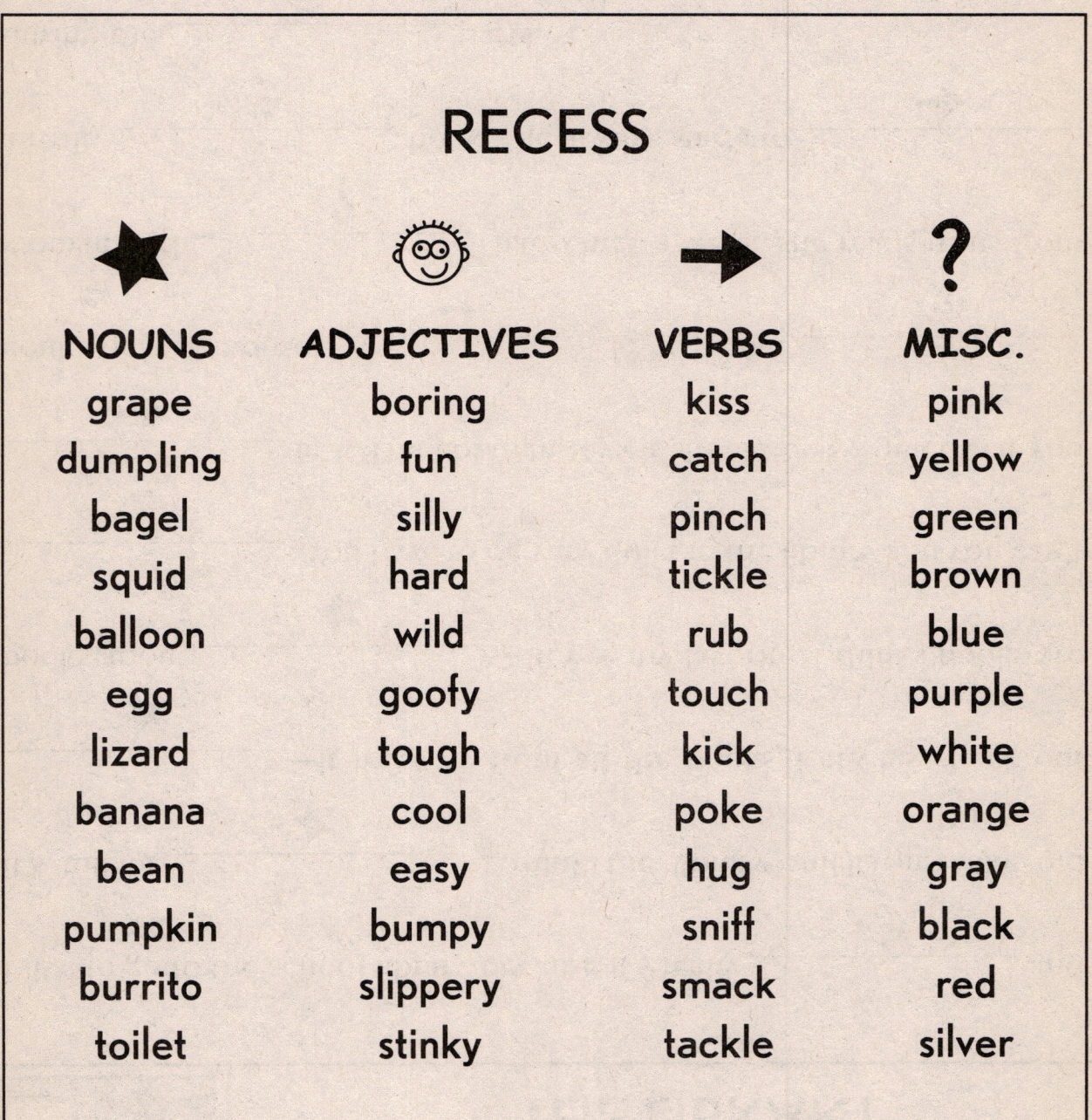

RECESS

★ NOUNS	☺ ADJECTIVES	➜ VERBS	? MISC.
grape	boring	kiss	pink
dumpling	fun	catch	yellow
bagel	silly	pinch	green
squid	hard	tickle	brown
balloon	wild	rub	blue
egg	goofy	touch	purple
lizard	tough	kick	white
banana	cool	poke	orange
bean	easy	hug	gray
pumpkin	bumpy	sniff	black
burrito	slippery	smack	red
toilet	stinky	tackle	silver

MAD LIBS ⊙ JUNIOR
RECESS

Recess is my favorite part of the day—it's so _____!

Some days, the whole class plays a/an _____ game of

_____ ball. You play it with a/an _____

_____ ball. You have to _____ the ball,

then run as fast as you can to the bases. Each base is marked with a

rubber _____. If you _____ someone before

they get to the base, they're out. When you make it all the way around the

bases, you win a/an _____ for your team. Mark said I

looked like a big _____ when I ran, but I didn't care

because I won the game for my team!

MAD LIBS JUNIOR™ is fun to play with friends, but you can also play it by yourself! To begin, look at the story on the page below. When you come to a blank space in the story, look at the symbol that appears underneath. Then find the same symbol on this page and pick a word that appears below the symbol. Put that word in the blank space, and cross out the word, so you don't use it again. Continue doing this throughout the story until you've filled in all the spaces. Finally, read your story aloud and laugh!

ART CLASS

★ NOUNS	☺ ADJECTIVES	→ VERBS	? MISC.
flower	clever	screaming	brown
skunk	ugly	dancing	purple
sculpture	pretty	painting	orange
trash can	creative	skipping	yellow
robot	nice	singing	red
toilet	funny	farting	pink
pizza	special	sleeping	green
dinosaur	mean	sculpting	white
pumpkin	dumb	yelling	black
house	talented	burping	gold
boat	stinky	crying	blue
sardine	crazy	eating	silver

MAD LIBS JUNIOR
ART CLASS

My favorite class is art class. My teacher is really _____. She

has _____ hair and always smells like a _____. She
?   ★

says that anyone can become a/an _____ artist. My favorite things
                                        ☺

to do in art class are drawing and _____—sometimes I do
                                        ➡

both at once! My teacher thinks I'm pretty _____. Last week,
                                                ☺

the whole class made a huge _____ out of pipe cleaners
                                    ★

and Popsicle sticks. It was really _____ and they put it on
                                        ☺

display in the main hallway of our school. And this week, we each get to

paint a _____. I think I'll make mine _____
            ★   **?**

with _____ stripes.
        ?

MAD LIBS JUNIOR™ is fun to play with friends, but you can also play it by yourself! To begin, look at the story on the page below. When you come to a blank space in the story, look at the symbol that appears underneath. Then find the same symbol on this page and pick a word that appears below the symbol. Put that word in the blank space, and cross out the word, so you don't use it again. Continue doing this throughout the story until you've filled in all the spaces. Finally, read your story aloud and laugh!

SPELLING BEE

★	☺	➡	?
NOUNS	**ADJECTIVES**	**VERBS**	**MISC.**
ant	mean	talk	purple
tomato	nasty	laugh	brown
egg	pretty	breathe	green
pig	silly	smile	yellow
bug	wacky	fart	red
apple	smart	sneeze	blue
bat	boring	giggle	pink
mosquito	weird	burp	orange
mouse	goofy	scream	tan
duck	crazy	dance	silver
cat	clever	sweat	white
lizard	funny	babble	gray

MAD LIBS JUNIOR
SPELLING BEE

Every year, Eleanor Bean wins the _____ school spelling

bee. She's a really _____ girl who looks just like a/an

_____ in glasses. She reads the dictionary just for fun and

she always wears her bright _____ hair in two tight braids.

On the day of the spelling bee, I was so nervous that I could barely

_____. On my first turn, the judge said my word was

"_____." I looked at the audience and I started to

_____ like crazy. I could feel my face turning

_____ as I quickly said some letters. The judge gave

me a _____ look and said, "I'm sorry, that's incorrect!"

MAD LIBS JUNIOR™ is fun to play with friends, but you can also play it by yourself! To begin, look at the story on the page below. When you come to a blank space in the story, look at the symbol that appears underneath. Then find the same symbol on this page and pick a word that appears below the symbol. Put that word in the blank space, and cross out the word, so you don't use it again. Continue doing this throughout the story until you've filled in all the spaces. Finally, read your story aloud and laugh!

THE SCHOOL NURSE

★ NOUNS	😊 ADJECTIVES	➡ VERBS	? MISC.
turnip	boring	cough	pink
pill	scary	choke	yellow
lollipop	nice	barf	green
meatloaf	mean	snort	brown
washcloth	funny	burp	blue
flower	round	hiccup	purple
olive	smelly	growl	white
cactus	friendly	sneeze	orange
pickle	lumpy	sweat	gray
onion	sweet	shake	black
cookie	prickly	fart	red
bucket	pretty	sing	silver

One day, I was sitting in class when I started to _____ ➡️ like

crazy and turned _____ ❓. My teacher gave me a/an

_____ ⭐ and sent me to the school nurse. Our school nurse is

a _____ 😊 lady who wears _____ ❓ shoes. Everyone

calls her the _____ ⭐ because she's so _____ 😊. She

has one _____ ❓ eye and one _____ ❓ eye. When I

got there, she told me to _____ ➡️ a little and to stick out my

tongue. Then she gave me a glass of water and a/an _____ ⭐

and told me if I didn't feel better, I could go home. Going to the school

nurse isn't so _____ 😊, after all!

MAD LIBS JUNIOR™ is fun to play with friends, but you can also play it by yourself! To begin, look at the story on the page below. When you come to a blank space in the story, look at the symbol that appears underneath. Then find the same symbol on this page and pick a word that appears below the symbol. Put that word in the blank space, and cross out the word, so you don't use it again. Continue doing this throughout the story until you've filled in all the spaces. Finally, read your story aloud and laugh!

SCIENCE PROJECT

★ NOUNS	☺ ADJECTIVES	→ VERBS	? MISC.
plant	gross	laugh	purple
toilet	silly	shake	brown
potato	funny	sing	green
worm	nasty	rust	yellow
onion	smelly	cry	red
pencil	sick	dance	blue
sock	sticky	mold	pink
Popsicle	strange	whistle	orange
mushroom	crazy	stink	tan
tree	sad	fart	silver
sausage	stinky	melt	white
donut	stupid	scream	gray

MAD LIBS JUNIOR
SCIENCE PROJECT

This year, everyone in my class had to do a _____ science fair 😊

project. For my project, I decided to put an old _____ in the ★

refrigerator to see what would happen to it. After a few days, it started to

turn _____ and _____. I couldn't believe it—I'd
❓ ➡️

never seen anything so _____! After a full week, it started 😊

to look like a flattened _____ and smelled like a/an ★

_____. But all my _____ work paid off. At the
★ 😊

science fair, I won a special award for having a really _____ 😊

project. I even got a/an _____ ribbon that said "Super
❓

_____ Science Student" and a big trophy shaped like 😊

a/an _____!
★